Hop on the
A Common Sense Guide to Leadership

Second Edition

www.heidylafleur.com

Twitter @HeidyLaFleur   #ClueBus

Common Sense Leadership, LLC
Heidy LaFleur, CEO

To spark the belief that everyone can lead.
Everyone.
Dedicated to making YOU believe in YOU.

ISBN: 0692166971
ISBE 13: 978-0692166970

Testimonials

True testimony resides within those on the front lines & those with the experience, knowledge and practical application.

The most precious thing in the world is a child. Leading a school where children are always put first is something I can sense the minute I walk into a building. As an author and presenter, I get the opportunity to meet and work with leaders from all walks of life. When I walk into Heidy's school, its personality shines brightly, as does her book.
Heidy understands the power of servant leadership to guide her teachers to grow in their practice. The culture she creates is trusting, strong, hard-working and friendly. You can feel it the minute you arrive. Many smiles and much confidence walk through her hallways because of what she has led.
It is essential that the greatest teachers are in classrooms. Heidy's book will lead you on the path that is best for children. For that, I thank her!
-Julia Cook, Internationally Known National Award Winning Children's Author - Nationally-Recognized Parent Expert - Educator - Former School Counselor

It's never been a tougher time in education with the demands put on schools and educators. As school leaders scramble to stay on top of all the new demands, sometimes they overlook the simple common sense leadership principles that truly work and make a difference in people's lives. Heidy's book, Hop on the Clue Bus is a thought-provoking guide to help any school leader become an effective leader of PEOPLE! We all know that leadership is affecting change in people, but how do you do it and get the results you want and need? Read Heidy's book and follow her simple steps to Common Sense Leadership and you will be on a journey to success. Get on the Bus and join others like Heidy in making a huge impact in students and teachers lives. Thanks Heidy for opening yourself up and sharing your own personal stories that are heartfelt, so we all can improve from your experience.

-James Jones, MBA aka Jim "Basketball" Jones - National Youth Motivational Speaker and creator of We Are 1 Team Character Education Program

Hop on the Clue Bus is a refreshing reminder to ALL educators that we have leaders in education who are still driven and compassionate. Heidy reminds us that we are ALL responsible for "leading" by the way we choose to lead our lives and treat one another. It is up to us. Heidy gives us the encouragement and the tools to make this happen. She shares her Core Beliefs and demonstrates ways to implement them as a leader. She also reminds us to let our humanity show through AND provides teachers with language to help them articulate what THEY might need from THEIR leaders (because…. "It's all about the conversation.") Thank you, Heidy, for reminding all of us that Common Sense IS an acceptable resource in leadership that we DO have control over some things in life (ourselves and our dispositions) and that, together, we can accomplish ANYTHING.

– Laura Dahl, Music Teacher

Heidy has nailed it. This book is absolutely the most effective way to run a school and to live your life! As a social worker, I teach students that they can always adjust their attitude when there is a problem situation. It is truly amazing to have a leader who is always able to find the positives in situations and people. Living this way, Heidy has created an environment where people want to come to work. It is nice to know that we

are supported by her and that she is here to help us grow in our weak areas (because we all have them). If more people used Common Sense and "Hopped on the Clue Bus" the world would be a better place.
– Elisabeth Betancourt, School Social Worker

This is a sensational, motivational and thought-provoking book that will serve as an inspiration to anyone lucky enough to read it! This is not only a guide for everyday work, but for everyday life.
– Judy Mendoza, Abigail's mom

Get ready for a truly inspiring ride! In this book, Heidy provides AWESOME insight into what makes a person into a positive, productive and successful leader. Heidy reminds us that common sense NEEDS to play a role in leadership because it helps to shape the teams we lead. A ride on the "Clue Bus" will not soon be forgotten because the lessons you learn along the way will enhance your thinking and will make you a more effective and encouraging leader!
– Sarah Mueller, Kindergarten Teacher - Golden Apple Teacher

Mrs. LaFleur was the Assistant Principal at my children's elementary school. I was immediately drawn to the strength and kindness that illuminated from her. During the time she served at our school, she always had such an approachable demeanor. Whether you found yourself next to her on the playground, or needed a seat in her office, she was always available with a willingness to not only listen, but with an eagerness to work to resolve whatever issue may be at hand. Her commitment to each child at our school was so evident, she wasn't just an administrator with a title, she was one with us. For me personally, my children faced both classroom struggles and personal heartbreak. During those times, Mrs. LaFleur was

always a beacon of compassion, thoughtfulness, and encouragement to not only them, but to me as well. Our lives have been blessed with the gift of Heidy LaFleur.
- Deana Rife, Noah & Skylar's mom

Heidy is a truly amazing leader. Her positive attitude, compassion and determination are contagious! She is the perfect person to educate and inspire other leaders. Hop on the Clue Bus is filled with examples of what awesome leaders possess and ideas that can easily be implemented immediately. Hop on the Clue Bus is a must read for every leader looking to improve their leadership skills and strengthen their team. Thank you Heidy for reflecting upon past experiences, taking notes along the way, and sharing your leadership toolbox; your book will change so many lives!
- Amy D'Antonio, Special Education

Dedication

To my beautiful family who continues to believe in me.
I love you all so much!

To my Dream Team . . . although we are in different places,
our hearts will always be together.
Just keep swimming!

To my PLN . . . thank you for lifting me up daily!
#CelebratED

To all of you that understand that
kids come first every single day.
Continue to engage them, believe in them,
listen to them, laugh with them & love them.

The Bus Route

Leadership is the organization, management, motivation, expectations, relationships and the growth of *PEOPLE* and as leaders, we can never forget that.

Foreword

Every so often, the stars align just right and I am able to enjoy a chance "reunion" with someone who has a special place in my heart. On March 14, 2015, I was fortunate enough to reconnect with Heidy Pemsl at the Iowa State Boys Basketball Tournament where Heidy was watching her nephew compete for a state title. Our brief conversation reminded me of how this incredible woman has impacted me in such a positive way and has helped me develop my own professional qualities.

My relationship with Heidy goes back to the early 1990's when I coached her in volleyball at Wahlert High School in Dubuque. It was clear even then that there was something very special about her. She was, in every sense of the word, a "leader."

It comes as no surprise that Heidy has authored an outstanding book on leadership. Through my own experience as an athlete, teacher, coach, athletic director and now principal of a high school, I've been blessed to have interacted with some truly outstanding leaders. Through those interactions, I've come to my own understanding of the essence of leadership. For as long as I've known her, Heidy has exemplified those qualities.

Heidy is, in the truest sense of the term, a "servant leader." She has always taken responsibility for those she has led. As captain of our volleyball team her senior year, she willed to the state tournament a team that "on paper" had no business competing for any kind of championship. She did it by sending a message loud and clear to her teammates that she believed in each and every one of them and that she would do whatever it took to help them develop into the kind of competitors who could indeed vie for championships. Because she believed in them, they believed in her.

A bona fide leader leads by example and leads with integrity. This was simply part of Heidy's DNA. She never expected anything from others – her coaches, her teachers, her teammates, her friends, her family – that she did not expect of herself. If she wanted greater effort from teammates, she ramped up her own effort (which was off the charts already!). If she wanted a positive environment, she created it with her own enthusiasm and encouragement. We could always count on Heidy to do the right thing – whether anyone was watching or not – simply because it was the right thing to do.

A leader shares the gifts he or she has been blessed with. Heidy believed that it was her responsibility to use her athletic ability not for personal accolades but for the success of her teams. More importantly, she used it to simply not allow her teammates to fail. Whether it was running down an errant pass, finding a way to attack a less than perfect set or launching her body toward the floor to dig a ball that got by a block, her teammates knew that Heidy "had their back."

A critical element of leadership is humility. Even as a teenager, Heidy knew the importance of directing compliments away from herself and toward her teammates. She realized that opponents deserved praise for their performances and for challenging her and her teammates. In a world of swag and chest-thumping, Heidy was a breath of fresh air.

Most importantly, the best leaders I've encountered lead from a position of unconditional love. Whether a teacher who loves students, a coach who loves athletes, a director who loves performers or a captain who loves teammates, the true leader feels an emotional connection to those he or she leads. There was never any doubt that Heidy's leadership was, at its core, a demonstration of love for those she led. We could hear it in her voice. We could see it in her eyes. We could feel it in her touch. True leaders understand that, "it's not about them." They focus their efforts on others. The true leader takes great satisfaction in the accomplishments of those they lead. I saw Heidy experience the exhilaration of conference and state championships earned. But the joy I witnessed when her teammates succeeded – individually and collectively – was something to behold.

I am so happy that Heidy has chosen to share her "common sense" guide to leadership with the world. Her perspective is one that will benefit all of us and if we take her words to heart, will benefit those we have been called to lead. From the moment I met her, I have grown to love Heidy Pemsl for the phenomenal human being she is. After reading, Hop on the Clue Bus, you'll understand why.

Tom Keating, President
Xavier High School

PREFACE

It seems that in some places of work and life, people are happy, willing, motivated, driven, positive and productive. Yet in other places, people are miserable, depressed, frustrated and noncompliant. Leadership has an awful lot to do with the way people feel. As I reflect on my career thus far, it all comes down to loving people, listening to people and finding ways to lift people to their highest potential. As the years have come and gone, and I have worked with different leaders, I have learned that leadership is a magical experience when the right people are at the helm and a nightmare when they aren't.

Magical leaders make people want to work and are looked up to for advice, strength and approval. Magical leaders are consistent, compassionate and strike a balance between fun and high expectations. Magical leaders are not afraid to show that they are human and make mistakes. Magical leaders celebrate others, often and follow through…always. They are the ones we are drawn to and they see talents in us even when we don't see them in ourselves. They push us, love us and believe in us. They offer the gift of confidence in us when we are ready to give up on ourselves.

I want to say that magical leadership is common sense, but I have realized that common sense is not very common. Some leaders are selfish. Some are focused on things other than people. Some leaders are worried too much about what others think of them or their own status. Some will walk all over others to get to the top. Some leaders look down upon people while preaching from up top and worst of all, is when politics lead the leadership. Ugh.

However, some work to build relationships with people. It's all about people. It's about finding strengths in individual people and making them into a team. Period. Some are awesome at this and others not so much. True leadership is the organization, management, motivation, expectations, relationships and the growth of PEOPLE and the best leaders never forget this.

I have been blessed with leaders in my life from which I have taken notes on things I have put in my leadership tool box. Thank you, mom for making me believe I was the best and that I could do anything. I know you are looking down on me every day with a proud smile. Thank you, Mr. Mac, for telling me in 2nd grade that I was the best kickball player in the world. Thank you, Mr. Draus, for moving me into the Blue Dolphins high reading group because you said I was ready for a challenge. Thank you, Mrs. Wilgenbush, for having such high expectations in junior high that we were afraid to let you down. Thank you, Mr. Keating, for coaching us to two state championships and demanding nothing but the very best at every practice, every game and in the classroom. You made us believe that there was no one that was going to beat us. Thank you, Mr. Sampson, for being on my side when the going got tough junior year.

Thank you, Coach, for putting me in the varsity game as a freshman in the bottom on the 9th inning being down 2-0 with 2 outs. I struck out, but I took notes. Thank you, as well, for taking me out of the clean-up spot in the lineup after I broke the home run record. I didn't understand, but I took notes. Thank you, Coach, for making us weigh in after you fed us pizza and yelled out our weight in front of the football players telling us that we were all too fat. I was angry, but I took notes. Thank you, Assistant Principal, for making up my observations and not providing me with any opportunity to talk about my growth as a teacher. I survived but I took notes. Thank you, Principal, for writing me up as a teacher for having a coffee pot in my room, even though I didn't drink coffee and it was the teacher next door to me. I was bummed, but I took notes. Thank you, other Principal, for giving me a needs improvement in attendance because I only achieved 95% the year my mother was dying of cancer. I was scared, but I took notes. Thank you, large school district, for creating a program for principals that sent me through tests and interviews and said I wasn't qualified to be a principal. After 14 years of excellent service to kids and colleagues, you chewed me up and spit me out, but I took notes. Thank you Superintendent for confronting me with a laundry list of lies and telling me I was defensive when my integrity was questioned. Thank you for questioning my work ethic and beating me down each time we spoke. You had no idea who I was, who I am or what I'm about. Your words and constant disbelief in me shook me, but I took notes.

I have learned from the most inspirational and amazing leaders and from among the worst leaders ever. From each, I have taken notes along the way and developed my own style of magic that is based on common sense and I would like to share it with all of you. So come on...Hop on the Clue Bus with me! Bring your friends! Let's change the world together...one kid at a time!

Heidy LaFleur

MY WHY

I hope my achievements in life shall be these...that I will have fought for what was right and fair, that I will have risked for that which mattered, that I will have given help to those who were in need...that I have left the earth a better place for what I've done and who I've been.

- C. Hoppe

Introduction

The idea sparked as I sat, nine months pregnant, in my final master's class back in 2003. We were discussing teacher evaluation and I started to jot notes. In my head, I thought many things. I was surprised at the way people were talking about people. You see, my classmates were sharing their views on teachers, on people. My whole life had been spent on teams and developing skills to deal with all different kinds of people. I was a problem solver and obsessed with finding success not only for myself, but for those surrounding me. I was hearing people talk about how easy leadership was and how a top-down approach is always best. Like many times then and now, I sat back and observed. I listened. I took notes. I imagined what my school would be like. I dreamed about helping teachers and kids and couldn't wait. There were so many classmates who didn't seem to understand that leadership is all about people. Leadership is about organization, management, motivation, expectations, relationships and the growth of PEOPLE. During that class, one of the things I jotted in my notebook was, "Some of these people need to get a clue," and that is where the title was born. I am a very realistic, no nonsense person. I wrote that as a thought and a belief. It is not to be confused with a put down as I am not about that, but I am however, about reality.

As professionals and leaders, we read so much on research & theory and all of it is relevant and important in developing our philosophies. I always felt, however, that we were missing discussion on common sense. Someday, I would love to create and teach a Common Sense Leadership course in college. What a perfect addition it would be to School Finance, Leaders as Change Agents and Leadership & Organization. Imagine a course that would help you make all of those better because you understand people. For example, you can talk to someone who knows a million leadership theories, but isn't an effective leader. Some will study and do well in school, but in the real world they flounder. I often asked myself what was it that I felt was missing from all of my classes. I remember sitting in some classes thinking, "Ah, this is such crap. What is it really like?" Well, this book will tell you what it's really like. It will tell you the importance of common sense and taking care of people. It will tell you how difficult conversations and honesty will make your team stronger. It will tell you that the most respected leaders put people first, talk the talk AND walk the walk. Respected and effective leaders honor people, guide people and listen to people. Never mistake this "soft" approach as weakness. In fact, this approach is difficult and draining at times, but worth every minute. This book will also share that you will not always be blessed with an amazing leader. Many of us have been broken down by our leaders, including me. However, as the Japanese Proverb states, I will fall down seven times and get up eight.

Just as a principal must lead teachers, teachers must lead students. All of the leadership qualities of effective leaders are the same in the classroom with teachers. The teachers who have the greatest impact on students are those who build relationships with their kids. They get to know them and help them grow. They do what it takes to understand how to motivate them, guide them and help them find success in and out of the classroom. What teachers do you remember? I remember the teachers who cared about me as not only Heidy the student, but as Heidy the child, adolescent, teenager and young adult. I remember the teachers who asked me about a game, about colleges, about my life. I know they taught me academics, but those who made a true impact went way beyond fractions and diagramming sentences. This, to me, is the difference in life. Each one of us has the ability to make life a little easier for someone else; because God knows life can be very difficult.

Who are the leaders in your life that you respect? What is it about them that you respect? On the other side of the token, why are some of you miserable, frustrated and held back? People are interesting and those on the bus will lift you up and make you want to work hard. They will inspire you, believe in you and trust in your abilities. Those not on the bus, will tear you down word-by-word and action-by-action. They will make your life difficult. Always know that you are amazing, you do make a difference and don't ever let anyone tell you otherwise. The second release of Hop on the Clue Bus has been written because when you work with someone who tears you down, it opens up many doors for you if you are willing to look. Never allow someone to tear you down without climbing right back up. You are worth it.

I challenge each of you, regardless of your title, to be a leader. Each time you read the word leader in this book, insert your position, because truly we are all leaders if we choose to be. This book is not just for educators, it is for all people who challenge the status quo. This book talks through an education lense because that is my experience. However, my background is building people, teams, challengers, disruptors, and questioning anything that gets in the way of making experiences positive for children.

For all of you, my wish is that you get to experience second-to-none leadership and you are lifted up and honored in the work you do. I also wish for leaders everywhere, to take a step back and reflect on how you can make someone's life a little easier…

All the Best,
Heidy

1

FRUSTRATION

"Frustration, although quite painful at times, is a very positive and essential part of success."

-Bo Bennett

You may wonder why I'm beginning at the bus stop on frustration, but common sense tells us that we all feel it. The positive leaders, the negative leaders, the common sense leaders all experience levels of frustration. When you feel, as a leader, that you are drowning in work and you feel like you have no control about what is happening in your school or in your life, it is beyond frustrating.

You are, however in control. You are in control of your thoughts and your mind. You are in control of your attitude and the way you present yourself to others. You are in control of how you treat people and how much time you devote to people. Is the glass half empty or half full? As a common sense leader, I know that my outlook and attitude control my perspective on all things. I also know that I have the power to be better and common sense leaders never stop learning.

Throughout my career, I have learned that life is a roller coaster. It's so fun and so scary. It's so easy and so hard. We all go through some great times and we all go through tough times. All people will go through something really difficult. It's not a matter of if; it's a matter of when. Some of the things that get us through both are family, friends and our attitude. The only common factor among the three is attitude. Some of us don't have a lot of family or friends, but we all have an attitude. Common sense leadership helps me remind others that at school and in life, people's attitudes are developed by their surroundings. We have so much power as leaders to form the attitude and actions of others. It takes time, but it is possible to help develop the positive in people. Positive people create a successful, thriving climate. The more positive support I spread as a leader, the more people will follow me...The more we will get done...The more effectively we develop children to their fullest potential. Understand however, that no matter how amazing or positive you are, some people will not get on board. But guess what? That's ok because you are not fighting for those people anyway. You are fighting for those who put kids first, who lift up your staff and your community. Ultimately you are fighting for those who are leading from any position. You don't have to have the title of leader to lead. Life is not about titles, it is about doing what you can for the team. The most effective teams lead from every position on the field.

On every team, frustration happens. It's just a part of life, but how we handle frustration is what makes the difference. When speaking while frustrated, I find it extremely important to remember that I have no idea what someone may be going through. A mentor once told me to never quit my job in the spring because frustration hits hard when school is about to end each year. He also reminded me that when frustrated, I may be tempted to say something that feels great in the moment and will be regretted an hour later. His advice was, "Be smart and if it feels good in the moment, don't say it!"

Working in a large urban district for fourteen years brought a great deal of frustration, but I took notes. I worked my butt off as a fourth grade teacher. I stayed late. I individualized for my kids. I wrote my own assessments. I had positive growth results with my students, but I was still frustrated. A few years after I started, my principal asked me to teach sixth and seventh grade math and I accepted the challenge. I prepared by studying student data, I formed groups, facilitated learning with guided note taking and grew kids in math, yet the parents received a letter stating that I was not "highly qualified." Ask the students, the parents, my principal and my colleagues if I was highly qualified. They are the ones who will be able to tell you. I learned that what mattered most was my preparation, planning, attitude, and the amazing growth of the kids; not the politics. #Frustrated

A few years later, I accepted the assistant principal position at the same school. I was so ready and excited. I now felt that I could not only help shape a classroom of 30 students, but a whole school of teachers. My mission was to get into the classrooms and be a true instructional leader. What would be better than helping teachers be the best teachers they can be? I was motivated to guide and help lower achieving teachers either along the road to improvement, or to move them out. If you've had the opportunity to observe poor instruction, you know what I mean. Too often, people don't exhibit the courage to have those tough conversations with teachers who struggle. Common sense tells us that if they are struggling, they may be doing harm in the classroom. I have the responsibility to help them improve. I also have the responsibility to work on getting them out if the help is not enough. Kids get one shot at school and we all need to be at the top of our game.

As a mother, I can't say enough about my children's teachers. Some have been unbelievable and others, well let's just say they are lucky not to be working in my building. Again, those of you who have had your children spend a year with a less than superior teacher know what I mean. For those who haven't seen poor instruction, don't worry, you will, and I challenge you to provide as much guidance as possible. If it doesn't work - do what you have to do to get excellent teachers in front of kids. The culture of your school will grow strong if you support those who excel and mentor those in need. Your culture will grow even stronger and more respectful if you follow through with tough conversations and hold people accountable to offer the best for kids.

In the school, our principal was overwhelmed with requests from the district, budget deadlines, faxes (yes, faxes!) that came in with due dates of three days ago, changing leadership and conflicting philosophies. She felt she was never able to go into the classrooms and be a true instructional leader. Though not her fault, we were on our own. Common sense would say that putting insane demands on a principal of a school and expecting amazing results is silly. Common sense would say that cramming 30 or more students into a classroom and expecting all kids to learn is ridiculous. Common sense would say that changing philosophy, CEOs, and expectations will not keep people above water. Common sense tells us that when the demand is greater than the supply, things are not going to get done well. It's frustrating to be a part of that, but again, we have control of our attitude and actions. We worked together to do what was best for kids and families. We didn't let the ridiculousness get in the way. It's not worth it.

When I was a senior in high school, I was the only returning starter on both the Varsity volleyball and basketball teams. Mr. Keating asked a former player, Kari Hamel, for some advice and she said – Be a part of the solution, not a part of the problem. Mr. Keating shared that with me and I share it everywhere I go. It is amazing advice. It is very simple. If you change your perspective, anything is possible. I came across the note he wrote me and I'd like to share it with you:

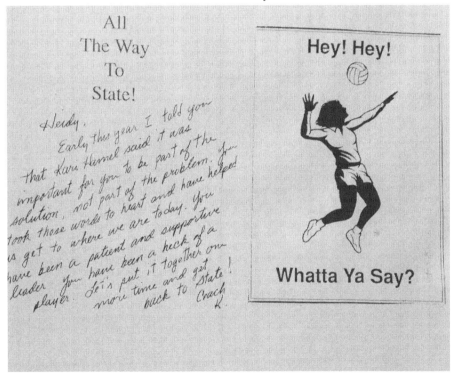

Mr. Keating took the time to write a note to appreciate and motivate me. Things like this truly make a difference. He certainly made a difference in my life.

It's a choice – be a part of the solution or be a part of the problem. Things can be very frustrating at times and God knows some of our buildings have poor leadership, but do what you can to be a part of the solution.

I was very fortunate to work at an amazing school in a large urban district. The staff and families were wonderful. The students were eager to learn and brought such joy to the school community. It's unfortunate that this district gets such a bad name at times, because there are so many amazing people doing so many amazing things with children. At the end of the day, the kids are what matters.

In order to drive through the frustration that comes with leadership and life, I live by a quote from C. Hoppe. My mother gave me a card when I was 16 years old and this quote was on the front. I can tell you that at 16, I didn't appreciate it like I do today. This quote reminded me how to deal with the bureaucracy of large entities and continues to help me each and every day:

> I hope my achievements in life shall be these...that I will have fought for what was right and fair, that I will have risked for that which mattered, that I will have given help to those who were in need...that I have left the earth a better place for what I've done and who I've been.
>
> - C. Hoppe

Regardless of the frustration that educational regulations - No Child Left Behind, Common Core, PARCC - can bring, I am the Master of my Fate and the Captain of my Soul. It is my job to help teachers help kids every day. It doesn't matter what the latest mandate is. Help them grow. Ignore the nonsense. Enjoy the moment. End of story.

The politics of education will always be there, but we have control over how we deal with it. No one can take away what we do in schools and in classrooms with students each day. I find honor in the fact that my words and actions shape the culture which shapes the climate of the school. I find honor in helping teachers be the best they can be. I find honor in open and honest conversations. Mostly, I find honor in opening up and allowing people into my life so they are never growing as educators next to a stranger. One of the most satisfying things in the world is a conversation with a teacher, student or parent in which you listen to each other and build the relationship that ultimately makes everything worth it.

Beginning my college student/athlete experience as a Division I volleyball player, I was overcome with frustration. I learned a whole lot of what not to do in leadership. I went from a State Championship and nationally-ranked high school program of belief and power, to a college program of put-downs, outrageous workouts and negativity. When I arrived as a freshman, the seniors were burned out before pre-season began. At our first team dinner, one of the seniors came to me and asked if I was homesick. I told her I was and she said, "Well good luck, because at this place it doesn't get any better." Yikes. How could she have said that? What kind of culture was I walking into? I was positive and ready. I wasn't going to get beat by anyone and I was a winner...or so I thought. The coach made fun of me because I was Catholic. What? What was wrong with that? That's all I knew coming from Dubuque, Iowa. *If you grew up in Dubuque, Iowa, you will know exactly what I mean!*

She would talk about girls' bodies and make fun of people on our team. There was no vision. There was no cohesive unit. There was no motivation. It was brutal. After three-hour conditioning practices, we would have to run a mile in under seven minutes or we had to do it again. It was by the grace of God that I ran that thing under seven minutes every time. She would then make us weigh in and if she didn't like what the scale said, we would work out more. I certainly wish I was as "fat" now as I was then!

I didn't have the motivation to impress. None of it made sense to me. There was no focus on team or individual growth. I didn't have the drive to make her proud because it didn't matter. It felt horrible. For three years, I continued to tell myself, however, that I wasn't going to feel or act like the seniors did. Although I tried very hard, four years later it happened. I just wanted to get out and be done. A sport that I loved and was so passionate about had become a chore. Facing that leader on a daily basis was enough to make me nauseous. There was no vision. There was no plan. There was no pride.

I learned a lot from her. Never lead without a backbone. Listen to your people. Believe in them and get to know them. Make them feel like they are on top of the world and they will work hard for you. Common sense tells us that frustration comes in many forms, and as leaders, we have the power to make everything palatable for our teachers. It's all in the presentation. The presentation is very powerful.

I left college with a sour taste, determined to make a difference with people…

"Common sense is genius dressed in its working clothes."

-Ralph Waldo Emerson

2

SHHH, LISTEN!

"One of the most sincere forms of respect is actually listening to what another has to say."

- Bryant H. McGill

Those of us blessed with the sense of hearing should know that listening is one of the most powerful things in the world. Hiring the right people and investing the time to listen to them is crucial to begin or continue your common sense journey. I enjoy interviewing teacher candidates because I learn so many things by listening to what they share with me. Interviews, to me, are one of the best times to sit back and learn about people. I learn about what other schools are doing to move their schools and their students forward. I also hear the brutal mistakes schools are making and wonder to myself, wow, what are people thinking? I learn about how people act when they are anxious and under pressure. I learn, through listening, how positive and productive individuals are. I learn if they can be problem solvers. Think about the difference you can make at an interview. As a leader, you can drill questions and expect to hear what you want to hear or you can sit at the table together and allow the candidate to discuss and share their value. Every person has something to offer and you should take mental notes as you interview. You never know when someone else's words will come in handy.

Working in a school setting with adults and children provides numerous opportunities to listen. Magical leaders listen with their entire bodies. They get on their hands and knees with kindergarten students and sit knee to knee with teachers and parents. They take their desk out of the equation to remove the barrier that separates the hierarchy of position. Magical leaders take time for people, listen to people and allow people time to be heard. They take time for parents too. Sometimes when a parent comes in screaming injustice regarding their child, they just want someone to listen. Some leaders start fuming and get into a battle of words. Common sense leaders take a deep breath and know that the parent is frustrated, upset and needs an outlet. Sometimes as leaders, that is exactly what we are. We are an outlet for students, teachers and parents. I'm not saying it's easy to take, or listen to, I'm just saying it's a common sense fact.

Leaders are honored when things are going well and blamed when things go poorly. Common sense leaders stay the course, listen to their players and take mental notes. They devise a plan with the input of the team in order to achieve success. Listening to your team is one of the most effective outcomes of common sense leadership. Your teams of teachers are in the classrooms, with the students all day. Who could possibly know more about what needs to happen and suggest how to make things happen? As a common sense leader, you will learn a lot about your teachers if you listen to them. Some of their input you will seek right away, some of their input will be put on a shelf for later and some of their input you will simply ignore. But the fact is, you listened. If people feel valued, they will work hard. If people know you genuinely listen to them, they will work hard. As the saying goes, those who feel appreciated will always do more than expected. To me, this is common sense, but it isn't to everyone.

In all of my experiences, I have come to the common sense conclusion that if we not only listen, but listen well, it will make a world of difference. People have great ideas. People want feedback. The vast majority of people work so hard and want to succeed. It seems that many decisions are made without thoughtful listening and planning. We are surrounded with expertise. Shh, just listen. We are surrounded with people who are ready for the next step. Shh, just listen. The true leaders find strength in EVERY team member and put them to work. Finding strength in your team means that you paid attention to them and listened to them. It works...I promise!

Too many times I have seen leaders make decisions without consulting with other team members. Common sense tells us that successful teams talk together and respect each other's work. As leaders, we have what it takes to make that happen. We lead it. We facilitate it. We participate and praise it. Over time, our teachers will see that we have been listening. It is amazing when it all comes together. In a smoothly run system, people feel valued and heard. People feel safe to take risks. People are grateful, motivated and determined to do their best. They are there, just listen to them.

Unless I have a confidential phone call or meeting, my door is literally open...always. Teachers know they are welcome to come in and talk and I will listen. They also know that if they come in with a complaint, that I expect they include a possible solution. That allows us to problem solve together. If you have an issue with something, it's fine by me, but know that I will expect that you share a way to solve the problem. By the way, has anyone ever asked you, "Do you have a minute?" That was a joke. I hope you laughed.

Listening to others isn't always an easy thing. Sometimes I feel like I help solve everyone's problems and it's exhausting. I think, man, I have enough issues in my life to worry about. However, I truly try to live by the C. Hoppe quote. I do all that it takes to make each day the best it can be so when it's time to bow out of this life, I will be able to do so with pride and integrity that I did all I could do to make things right. Every night before I go to bed I think about whether or not I lived my why. Some days I do great. Other days I know I could have done better. But after all, listening to ourselves and reflecting on our practice makes a difference as well.

Take the time to listen to people; it will make a difference…

"The word LISTEN contains the same letters as the word SILENT."

-Alfred Brendel

3
COMMUNICATION & MOTIVATION

"The art of communication is the language of leadership."

-James Humes

There's nothing like trying to get somewhere without a map. It never works very well. One of the most crucial elements of common sense leadership is that you need a map and you must share it with your teachers. Open communication will keep everyone out of the dark. The dark is a very scary place to be when you are looking for guidance. If a leader doesn't know where he/she is going, then the followers will have no clue. Having no clue leads to frustration, anger and resentment; three things that can ruin school culture very quickly.

Knowing your why and remembering it each and every day will help develop your map. Sometimes we get so busy with the day-to-day work, that our why gets fuzzy and we lose focus. Your why is something that should be kept close at all times, posted and read often. Never underestimate the importance of why you do what you do. It will be something you turn to when life takes you on a wild ride of reality. Like I shared earlier, unfortunate events happen to all of us. It's not a matter of what, it's a matter of when. Your why will keep your words and actions in check and will drag you out of any place you may get stuck. Simply ask yourself, why do I do this everyday? From there, your map will seem a lot more clear.

As a leader, having vision of where you want to take your school is one thing, but actually communicating that vision to others is another. Common sense leadership is developing your vision and talking about it all of the time. Everything that happens in your school must be driven by the vision. If a clear vision has been established and communicated, your teachers will know where they are going. They will work hard and focus on that vision because they are reminded through your verbal and written communication that it is at the forefront of decision-making. Your actions as a leader will motivate them to be the very best they can be. Common sense tells us that motivation comes from both within each of us and from what our leaders tell us & how they treat us. I believe that if someone is doing well, they should hear it from me. Successful leaders send motivational emails, tweets, notes, cards and sometimes even small gifts. If teachers know that you see their efforts, they will believe in the vision and work hard. I also believe that when teachers aren't living up to my expectations, I need to do the same. Sending a note, a card or an email reminding the teacher of our vision and offering a hand or an ear can go a very long way in making sure the entire team is on the same page. Words are very powerful. Communication is key. Common sense leaders communicate when things are going beautifully AND when things are slipping.

I will always remember the week before every high school volleyball match; Mr. Keating would give us the scouting report. He created a document showing the rotation of players of the team we were playing. In each rotation, he would tell us what the team was doing and where we could attack. He shared percentages of where their hitters hit and where they served. He matched our line-up to best meet theirs and repeated our vision over and over. We were prepared. The vision of Wahlert High School volleyball was that we were going to win - hands down. Through his verbal and written communication, we believed that we worked harder, we practiced harder and we were going to win every match - no questions asked. Mr. Keating was organized. He had a vision. He lived it. He communicated it. He made us believe and it worked. The confidence bestowed upon us was a true gift at that time and throughout our lives. Wahlert volleyball was a nationally-known program. We knew it and lived it. It was an honor to wear the blue and gold uniform.

In the 1992 State Volleyball Championship in Cedar Rapids, Iowa, I was a sophomore starter and we were playing Hull Western Christian in the championship match. We knew the vision. We were prepared and confident that the vision would be sealed that night. Little did we know that we would be down two games to none in a very short time. I remember a few of the upperclassmen getting so upset on the court. They were saying that the refs did not want us to win because all of the calls were going against us. They were hitting balls way out of bounds and serving into the net. Our team was losing sight of the vision. All that we had worked for was slowly blurring and unfamiliarity was overcoming us. I had never been part of something so important to me and it felt like it was slipping away.

After the second match, we ran into the locker room and sat down. No one said much and the pit in my stomach grew bigger. My teammates had their heads down and I had never seen that before. Mr. Keating usually came in all fired up either telling us to get our heads out of our butts or praising us to continue in the manner that we were. This time was different. The communication he used was among the most powerful I have ever experienced. He took our blurred minds and refocused us by uniquely sharing the vision we lived by.

Mr. Keating walked calmly into the locker room and said:

> Out of the night that covers me,
> Black as the pit from pole to pole,
> I thank whatever gods may be
> For my unconquerable soul.
>
> In the fell clutch of circumstance
> I have not winced nor cried aloud.
> Under the bludgeonings of chance
> My head is bloody, but unbowed.
>
> Beyond this place of wrath and tears
> Looms but the Horror of the shade,
> And yet the menace of the years
> Finds and shall find me unafraid.
>
> It matters not how strait the gate,
> How charged with punishments the scroll,
> **I am the master of my fate,**
> **I am the captain of my soul.**

He was passionate. He was real. He was communicating that we were in control of our fate. After reciting William Ernest Henley's *Invictus*, he looked each of us in the eye and said, "If we are going down tonight, it better be with the best fight you have in you," and he walked out. We all stood up, looked at each other and came together in a circle. Someone said, "Let's go. Let's do this." We ran back out onto that court and won the next three games winning the State Championship. The match ended with me serving two aces to the front row. I went on to serve a million more balls in my career, but never in my life have I experienced such poise and confidence while serving a ball as I did that unforgettable night.

Mr. Keating's way of motivating us that evening is proof that the way a leader communicates is vital to the outcome. In a school, we strive for students to grow socially, emotionally and academically. We have the power to set a vision for the kids and teachers and make it happen. We have the power to communicate the vision in unique ways. We have the power to motivate our teachers and students by taking the time to get to know each and every one of them as best we can. Common sense leadership will never go wrong. Hop on the Clue Bus...the more of you we get on the bus, the better off we will be and the more success stories we will read.

I find myself communicating with parents through tweets, notes, emails and postcards about their kids' successes. I also find myself thanking parents for all they do for their children...here's why:

2005 KANE ST.
DUBUQUE, IOWA 52001

Tom Keating
Head Coach
W (319) 583-9771
Fax 319-583-9775
H (319) 557-1366

Assistants
Jim Kuhl
Jan Thyne
Deb Norman

Gene Pierotti
Athletic Director

Don Miller
Principal

State
Tournament
Appearances

1973
1974
1976
1977
1978
1981
1982
1985
1986
1987
1989
1990
1991
1992
1993

November 14, 1993

Dear Dave and Linda,

Just a short note to let you know how much I've truly enjoyed the opportunity to work with Heidy these past three years. She has been a credit to Wahlert Volleyball and a credit to Wahlert High School.

Without a doubt, Heidy is the best leader I've had in my coaching career. I've had players who've collected more awards and accolades, but I've never had a young lady who was so willing to give her time and effort to her teammates. Heidy is one of the few athletes I know who is capable of putting her own concerns aside for the sake of her team.

As captain, Heidy did a remarkable job of keeping this team focused on what was important. It was no accident that we were able to succeed despite the differences in age and interests of our players. Heidy did everything in her power to make sure that each player felt she was an important part of this group.

We've all seen what a terrific player Heidy has become. What I am more impressed with, however, is the type of person Heidy has become. Never in my career have I had a player I was more willing to trust. Heidy knows the difference between right and wrong. She has made the choice to do what's right. That, as we know, is not always the popular choice. As a result, Heidy is one of the best role models to ever come through the Wahlert program. Our younger players truly admire and respect her. She has had a tremendous impact on them.

I think I've seen enough high school students and coached enough athletes to know that they don't turn out the way they do by accident. Heidy is who she is, in large part, because of the way you've raised her. As they say, "The nut doesn't fall far from the tree." Heidy is lucky to have parents who care enough about her to set rules she must live by. She is lucky to have parents who care enough about her to support her in all she does. And I want you to know that she appreciates you.

I want to thank you personally for all you've done for the Wahlert Volleyball program these past four years. Whether it was pizza at Shot Tower, an encouraging word when I needed it, food at a tournament, or a "Go Blue!" at just the right time, I truly appreciate you help.

Thank you so much for choosing to send Heidy to Wahlert. My experience with her has had a tremendous impact on my life. She has taught me a great deal about trust, commitment, hard work and persistence. I miss her already.

Sincerely,

Tom

Tom Keating

| State Champions | 1974 | '76 | '77 | '78 | '86 | '87 | '90 | '91 | '92 |
| MVC Champions | 1978 | '79 | '81 | '83 | '85 | '86 | '87 | '89 | '90 | '91 | '92 |

For my parents to receive such a beautiful letter about their daughter makes me so thankful. It also has helped me understand and act upon the fact that calling parents to share great news is totally awesome!

One of the most rewarding things is learning with kids in the classroom and seeing a student overcome an obstacle, give their best effort or offer something special to the class. It is those times I ask the student to take a walk with me and we call their parent. Telling the parent how amazing their child is may be one of the best parts of working with kids. The reaction, the pride and the smile that is felt through the phone are all things that motivate me, my parents and my students. Watching a child beam as I brag to his/her parent will not soon be forgotten by that child. If we are intentional about our communication and motivation, anything is possible. I am the Master of my Fate and the Captain of my Soul. You are too…

"You can't have a million-dollar dream with a minimum-wage work ethic."
-Stephen C. Hogan

4
HIGH EXPECTATIONS
WITH HUMAN TOUCH

"High expectations are the key to everything."

-Sam Walton

To me, there is little separation between my work and my personal life. I am who I am, regardless if it's a weekday during the school year, or a weekend day at home. My positive outlook is the same for my staff as it is for my family. I also share the fact that I am a human being, just like everyone else. At home, my family lives on the phrases, "The most important thing in the world is family," and "Be Awesome!" At school, we live on two phrases, "Our job is to make each day the very best day for every child," and "You are a professional. Just do it and do it well." The messages deliver the same expectations. Be the best you can be and take care of each other, every day, no matter what. If that attitude is in place and modeled, the school environment will thrive.

Common sense leadership tells us that our personality and attitude about humanity leak through in everything that we do. Teachers know leaders who talk the talk and also know those who walk the walk. Period. If you talk with no action, it will have a dramatic impact on the culture of your school or organization. Leaders must keep their word. People are relying on you and looking up to you for guidance and feedback. What we say is sacred to some. That sounds awfully pretentious, but it's not meant to be...it is simply the truth. People learn to love us or hate us and it really depends on how we treat them and how we package information. Students, teachers and athletes look up to good leaders. They want to impress them. They don't want to let them down. They want badly to improve and be recognized in the eyes of their leader. So what are you waiting for? Tell your best teachers how amazing they are. Recognize them and their efforts. Guide them to take leadership roles and go above and beyond to help kids grow. If they are working hard and hear it from you, I guarantee they will work even harder! Never miss an opportunity to tell someone you recognize their effort and excellence.

On the flip side, talk to those who are not living up to the expectations. Do not be afraid to do so. Helping those who struggle will make your school stronger and will grow the respect others have for you. There is nothing more degrading than the leader who writes "Excellent" evaluations for everyone. That's like a slap in the face to those who excel. Having difficult conversations with teachers is not easy. Following through on helping teachers who need improvement isn't easy. Common sense tells us that holding yourself and others to high expectations isn't easy either, but since when is good work easy? I encourage you to keep documentation on all of your teachers, but especially those who struggle. Student success depends on what kinds of teachers are in front of them. In my experience, effective teachers are motivated, determined, self-starters, responsible, leaders, problem solvers, team players, committed, fair, focused, passionate, nurturing, mature and possess a stellar work ethic. When you look at evaluating teachers, there are several things that stand out in excellent teachers. Not only do their students grow each year, but these teachers grow in their profession as well. They take constructive criticism and turn it into success. The most important quality in a successful teacher is their attitude. So many times excellent teachers will ask how they can improve. Sometimes I respond by saying that as long as your attitude and work ethic stay where they are, you will always improve and grow. We've all seen them...the teachers who go above and beyond. They are amazing and it shows in every aspect of evaluation. With that said, common sense tells us that not everyone is excellent. Leaders who have and model high expectations must do what it takes to get the best teachers in front of students every day. I take it upon myself to visit classrooms frequently and offer feedback to discuss. I also take it upon myself to hold people to what is expected. Like I said earlier, we are professionals. Just do it and do it well. If you don't, why bother?

In my experience, holding those who struggle to high expectations is draining. It can be painful and feel like a fight. You will feel resistance and it can be tense. It is uncomfortable and it is necessary, no matter how respectful you are. Our kids get one shot. One. Every child should be met with a motivated, determined, self-starting, responsible, leader, problem solver, team player, committed, fair, focused, passionate, nurturing, and mature teacher who possesses a second-to-none work ethic. It boils down to teachers believing in kids. Teachers telling kids they are amazing. Teachings planning innovative lessons to allow kids to be curious and dying to return the next day. Effective teachers are the most hard working and amazing people in the world. As a leader and a mother, I can not say enough about great teachers. Behind great teachers are common sense leaders there to believe in them, guide them, push them and help them take risks to get better. One of the greatest gifts a teacher can give a student is the gift of confidence. One of the greatest gifts a leader can give a teacher is confidence as well.

I've worked with many principals who didn't spend a lot of time in classrooms. They would write evaluations at the last minute and hand them to teachers as they walked out the door for summer break. What is that? The whole point behind observation is to help teachers grow. We all have the potential to be better and common sense leadership is a huge part of that. The best part of an evaluation cycle is the conversations I have with teachers. It is so awesome to hear teachers talk about what they want to see in their classrooms and I get to be a part of helping get them there. Cool stuff! This can be done! It takes a lot of time, but it is so worth it. Observing teachers and talking to them about their goals and student achievement is the best part of leadership. Having high expectations, helping teachers set goals and guiding them is such a powerful thing, yet it isn't done enough. If you want to make a true difference, set high expectations and live by them. Have empathy for people, but hold them accountable. Never underestimate the power of a meaningful conversation.

Together we deal with so many funny stories because we are dealing with kids. Kids say the funniest things and sharing those stories helps build relationships with each other. Keeping things on the lighter side helps with everything. No matter what mandate is next or what report is due, taking things in stride with a side of laughter goes a long way. Common sense tells us that people will feel comfortable sharing stories about kids when they feel safe to do so. Laughing together is an excellent way to let people know you are down to earth and a person who likes to have fun. You are leading with human touch. The last time I checked, we all put our pants on the same way. Leaders who don't have fun with their colleagues close doors to relationships and trust. Remember, part of helping people grow is showing that you are a regular person. Why do some leaders put themselves on a pedestal? It doesn't work well that way. Leaders who can relate to and talk with people are the most successful. Leaders who have difficulty breaking through the barrier and can't act real or laugh with their colleagues will have a hard time. It's a common sense fact.

The Golden Rule is true for everyone. Just as excellent doctors have stellar bedside manner, common sense leaders lead with human touch. Help when you can. Schedule creatively to make time for teams to meet. Listen when they need to be heard. Cover a class once in a while. Play music at the end of the day and invite them to dance in the hallways. Tell a joke on the intercom. Cancel a meeting when the team is tired or it's the first day of beautiful weather. There are many things we can do as leaders to ease the stress of the very difficult job of teaching students, yet honor high expectations. I hold myself to the very highest standards and expect that of others as well, however, at the forefront of my actions is leading with human touch. Life is short. Enjoy the people in your building. Enjoy the families. Enjoy the students. It's worth all of the time you spend. Leading with human touch and living in the moment are very important aspects of common sense leadership!

"People have forgotten what the human touch is, what it is to smile, for somebody to smile at them, somebody to recognize them, somebody to wish them well. The terrible thing is to be unwanted."

-Mother Teresa

5
COMPASSION & EMPATHY

"If your emotional abilities aren't in hand, if you don't have self-awareness, if you are not able to manage your distressing emotions, if you can't have empathy and have effective relationships, then no matter how smart you are, you are not going to get very far."

-Daniel Goleman

Standing in the principal's office, as her assistant, I will never forget the day when a teacher came in looking very upset. She said that she needed to call her husband because she was actively having a miscarriage. This was a teacher who had been at the school for a long time. She and her husband were having trouble getting pregnant and they were so excited that they finally were. The poor woman could hardly speak, but was trying to ask if someone could cover her class so she could call her husband. I told her no problem, that I would help her. The principal told her to go to her car, call her husband and come back in to teach. I was sick about that. It was 1:30 in the afternoon and this woman was going through a personal tragedy. I walked out of the office with her and told her to go home. I told her not to worry that I would cover her class for the rest of the day and that's what I did. I saw no other option.

I feel very strongly that walking in someone else's shoes and feeling what they may feel is very powerful. Being a common sense leader means taking care of your people. It means having compassion for their lives outside of school. We have and will continue to have so many opportunities to simply show love, compassion and empathy for people. When I was an assistant principal, we had a first grade student named Abigail whose neuroblastoma was in remission. She was the cutest little thing. Her therapy left her with wispy thin hair and hearing aids. Her mother was and is on the board of the American Childhood Cancer Association and showed me a fundraiser called Pjammin for Kids with Cancer. She asked if I would think about running the fundraiser and I couldn't wait to get started! Can you imagine having a child with cancer? Running a fundraiser at school is the least I could do to show kindness and compassion. It is now a tradition at that school to host Pjammin for Kids with Cancer to show support in fighting the disease! Compassion for people is an outstanding way to build the culture and climate of your school. This year, Abigail celebrated ten years cancer-free!

Dealing with people means dealing with death in families. It means dealing with teachers getting sick and taking leaves. It comes with sharing news with the staff that isn't always pleasant. Leaders are truly in powerful places. We deliver the good and the bad. We deliver happiness and sadness. The way in which we do so has a huge impact on our school and always will. It is when people are at their worst that they remember who you were to them. Were you an obstacle or a teammate? My job as a common sense leader is to take away any obstacle that gets in the way of teaching and learning. My job is to be a partner, a teammate and a friend at times.

My beautiful friend and old neighbor Shannon, lost her little girl to cancer five years ago. Leah and my son, Garrett went to preschool together and were the best of friends. Leah told everyone in the neighborhood that she was going to marry

Garrett. She was so proud and so was Garrett. Their friendship was so innocent and special. They would read together at school and put their arms around each other. Shannon is a teacher who had an amazing support group at her school. Her teaching colleagues helped her through so many difficult times. Think about the impact you have as a leader when tragedies strike your building. You can help. You can listen. You can make heartfelt efforts to encourage and strengthen the bonds of others. I am very thankful that many were on the bus at Shannon's school. Leah became an angel on 12-12-12 and I often feel that she waited for the stars to align for her. Shannon's empathetic and supportive colleagues do an annual fundraiser in honor of Leah. They get it.

I had an amazing paraprofessional who took in her pre-teenage cousin because her aunt was very sick and couldn't take care of her. This woman already had a small child at home and thought nothing of taking in her cousin so she could have a good life. When the time came for her aunt to pass, she stepped up even more gaining custody of the girl. Imagine the unselfishness. When her aunt was dying, she would feel terrible missing school and would worry about her students. I told her to never worry and to take care of herself and her family. I asked our staff to make donations for her and sent her a gift card telling her to use it to help ease the pain. When people are hurting and stressed, a little grocery money can go a long way. Anything to help ease the burden life brings to us at times.

When I was 22, my mother was diagnosed with colon cancer. She spent my college graduation day in the operating room experiencing a pelvic exenteration. She underwent years of treatment and fought the fight like nobody's business. She lost her hair several times and suffered burns from radiation. My mom would always say that there is someone out there who has it worse than she did. I would go visit her almost every weekend and sometimes take Friday afternoons off to make the three hour drive back home. It was so difficult being away from her. I will never forget getting my final evaluation that showed "needs improvement" in attendance because I was only present 95% of the time. Talk about lack of compassion. I was so mad about that because that leader never walked a minute in my shoes. It felt as if she didn't care. It felt as if she went on with her life as if nothing mattered and she showed no compassion to me. As a leader, I have learned to differentiate. You see, calling in sick for no good reason and being at school 95% of the time is one thing, but leaving half days to take care of your sick mother is another. Just like teachers have to differentiate in the classroom, common sense leaders have to differentiate as well. Fair isn't everyone getting the same thing. Fair is everyone getting what they need in order to be successful.

I made the trip a million times until I got pregnant with my first child and could no longer travel. Four weeks after Lilly was born, my mom was rushed to the Mayo Clinic in Rochester, Minnesota because they couldn't stop her bleeding. I bundled up my first born child, who was 28 days old, and drove in a snowstorm to see my mom. It was there in her hospital room that she looked me in the eye and said she was going to die. There I was, a new mom listening to my mom tell me that the end was near. I was 28 years old. My heart was sick. I stayed in a hotel in Minnesota with Lilly for two weeks. After that, my mom was transferred back home and was put on hospice. Lilly and I moved back home and my husband would come visit us on the weekends. During that time my mom grew weaker and weaker. She had a colostomy bag, nephrostomy tubes, and yet she still found a way to dig deep and be humorous up until a week before she died. We had to pack her wounds and take care of her. Taking care of my mom was one of the most painful, gut-wrenching experiences I have ever had. It was also one of the greatest honors in the world. My maternity leave was up and we decided that I would ask for a longer leave so I could help my mom die. That sounds strange, but those who have had a terminal parent, may understand what I mean.

Back at school during this time, I had one parent on the board tell the principal that she needed to stop hiring the "young chick-a-dees that get pregnant and extend their maternity leave." Her son was in my fourth grade class that year. People like that amaze me. Far from compassionate. That mother went on to nominate me for a Golden Apple Award for Teaching Excellence. Interesting how she thought I was such a great teacher for her son, but didn't possess the compassion to look at me as a person, a mother, and a grieving daughter.

On the evening of April 18, 2004, the date I was to report back to school, my mother passed away. It was so difficult, and yet so powerful. As I held my beautiful daughter and my family prayed together, the wind picked up like crazy and she took her last breath.

No card from my school. No flowers at her funeral. I was going through the greatest tragedy of my young life and the leadership did not walk in my shoes. Something to think about...

"If you want others to be happy, practice compassion. If you want to be happy, practice compassion."

-Dalai Lama

6
ORGANIZATION

"Your core values are the deeply held beliefs that authentically describe your soul."

- John C. Maxwell

Common Sense Leadership represents organization in many ways. Leading people effectively means that you, as the captain, have to know where you are going and have an idea & vision of how you are going to get there. Once there, you must have a plan to grow and change with the time, the people, the demands and the generation. Being organized means, in your thoughts and words, both verbal and written, you have cohesive thoughts and plans. You express them in a positive, honest and confident manner. You make people believe in you. You make people want to follow you and create a sense of curiosity in them. Organized leaders with common sense never lose their curiosity. They never grow old in their thoughts. They never allow their minds to get stale. They gain momentum and energy from others motivated to be the best and, in turn, motivate others to give their very best.

Organization starts with knowing who you are. You are who you are because of the influence of people. You are who you are because of your experiences. Do you know who you really are? When you know who you are, your core beliefs are born and when core beliefs are established, organized thoughts can start. When organized thoughts are in place, written plans can

begin. After written plans are drafted, the fun begins! Common
sense tells us to create a vision and leadership style based on all
that we have read, what we truly believe and what we have
experienced. Every leader has a different set of core beliefs and
execution plan for those beliefs. However, leaders on the Clue
Bus have a balance of confidence and humbleness about them.
You see, the best laid plans are not effective if no one believes in
you.

A few years into being an assistant principal, during a
professional development session, I was asked to write down
my core beliefs. At the time, it seemed like such a daunting
task, overwhelming to think about. Turns out, it was one of the
most beneficial and valuable exercises I have even been asked to
do. In fact, I find myself visiting that list often and streamlining
my thoughts and actions to those core beliefs. Writing down
what I truly thought about leadership and life began the
organization of my thoughts and vision of not only who I was,
but where they would take me.

Here is what I wrote:

My Core Beliefs:

> - *Honesty* – even when it is difficult
> - *Compassion* – walk in other people's shoes before
>   making decisions
> - *Work Ethic* – high expectations for self and others
> - Communicate – people who don't know can only
>   assume
> - *Appreciate* – recognize greatness and appreciate it

- ➢ *All Kids Can Learn* – regardless of what life has dealt, make it better for every child
- ➢ *Humor* – laugh, motivate, keep it real

After 10 more years in education and many more experiences, I redefined my list:

- ★ *Honesty* – even when it is difficult - it will help others grow
- ★ *Compassion* – walk in other people's shoes before making decisions & never get taken advantage of - make sure your kindness isn't mistaken for weakness
- ★ *Work Ethic* – high expectations for self and others - model with words and actions
- ★ *Communicate* – people who don't know can only assume - be consistent & to the point
- ★ *Appreciate* – recognize greatness, appreciate it, celebrate it
- ★ *All Kids Can Learn* – regardless of what life has dealt - make it better for every child - help others understand this
- ★ *Humor* – laugh, motivate, keep it real
- ★ *Never forget where I came from* - teacher first, always

I think about and refer back to these beliefs often. If you are going to be true to yourself and a common sense leader, you have to have a strong belief system of who you are, what you stand for and how you do business. Without a strong sense of self, how can you lead?

Everything I do involves my core beliefs; the way I talk, the way I communicate, the way I motivate and the way I carry &

organize myself. Most every teacher wants to do his/her best. They have very full plates each day and night. Their jobs don't end at 3:00 PM. They are planning lessons, buying supplies, grading papers, and creating projects well into the night. Trusting that they are putting forth the necessary effort to be successful, common sense tells me to take away any possible barriers to their success. Being an organized leader is the number one barrier that can be taken away. How can a teacher feel organized if their leader is not organized? Leaders chasing the Clue Bus never catch it because they can't follow it. They get lost and confused which causes their teachers to get lost and confused. This common sense chain now continues to the students. Imagine their learning environment when leaders and teachers are confused. Lack of organization equates to lack of progress and growth.

Written communication is vital to common sense organization. Common sense leaders need to find the "just right" amount of communication. I provide a monthly calendar to my staff, as well as a weekly memo reviewing the week's events, meetings and reminders. Often in the weekly memos you can find a funny cartoon related to the most recent events. You can find quotes to think about, articles to read for professional development and shout outs to staff members. In all that I produce, my core beliefs are expressed and you will see a pattern of that consistent belief system in the forms I use.

Another very important part of organization is establishing consistency. What do the memos look like? What can teachers expect? When can they expect the memos? Being upfront and establishing consistent communication guidelines will ease the expectation because question marks are removed. There is nothing worse than the unknown. The unknown often brings feelings that are over thought and boil over into unnecessary issues and drama that you don't have time for. I do everything I can to avoid unnecessary drama…I already spent four years in high school.

My goal is always to have teachers working on their art of teaching. I find it my job to make sure they have the science of teaching. I am responsible to get them curriculum, materials, supplies and professional development. I am responsible for helping guide teachers through data and make decisions, much like a teacher guiding her students with modeling and then a gradual release. The goal is to make students independent thinkers and that goal is no different for my teachers.

Make the time to reflect on yourself. On my website, www.heidylafleur.com, you will find a guide to help you think about those who influenced you throughout your life. You will find a place to write about and describe your core beliefs and lastly is a place to define your why. This activity is very powerful, grounding and a solid foundation to any leadership practice. I encourage you to give yourself the gift of taking time to reflect and revisit who you really are.

"For every minute spent organizing, an hour is earned."

- Benjamin Franklin

7
EVALUATION

"Before you are a leader, success is all about growing yourself. When you become a leader, success is all about growing others."

- Jack Welch

Evaluation is a difficult concept for many. Some people take it very personal and others take it as a challenge to improve. At the end of the day, evaluation should be a process where both the principal and teacher work together toward a goal. All of us have areas we can improve. What makes the difference is how that need for growth is approached.

Effective evaluation boils down to trust and relationships. If you don't trust your leader, you won't let your guard down to discuss areas of improvement. Instead, most people get defensive and angry because they don't feel their leader is listening. Taking the time and effort to accurately evaluate people is very hard work, even overwhelming at times. However, effective, fair and accurate evaluations will be held in the highest regard in your school.

At the beginning of my career, I worked at a Catholic School in Chicago for one year. I will never forget May 12, 2000. It was my first summative evaluation meeting with my principal. Before the meeting, there was one 15 minute walkthrough and one formal observation, none of which came with discussion, a pre or post conference or anything in writing. The first time I was observed was an informal "walk-in" in February which was 15 minutes long. I was conducting a 3rd grade math lesson on using vocabulary in word problems to determine which operation to use in order to find the solution. The second observation was the day before spring break. My principal was supposed to come at 10:00 AM. She arrived at 10:10 AM and stayed until 10:25 AM. Those were the only times she was in my classroom. It was my first year of teaching.

As I sat in the summative meeting, the principal told me that I was a born teacher. She said that I taught many higher order concepts to the kids. She then said that I could sign the evaluation and come back if I had any questions. When I arrived back in my classroom, I took a closer look at my evaluation. I cared a lot about what my boss thought about me and always wanted to impress. I found an overall wonderful rating, which I took great pride in - but then I read the comments. They read, "Ms. Pemsl has excellent rapport with parents, students and colleagues. She is aware of and responsive to students' individual needs. Heidy is generous and extending to the faculty. Ms. Pemsl needs to work on her personal attire. She needs to bare more regard to safety issues, and consult with administration before changing formats of school-wide documents!"

I pondered for awhile trying not to be angry, yet wondering what the principal was talking about. I decided to ask for a meeting to discuss her comments. As a first year teacher at this school I was a little scared, yet needed the principal to justify the comments. I wanted to grow as a teacher, so if I was doing something wrong, I wanted to know more about it.

One week later we sat down after school and the principal asked why I called the meeting. I shared that although I appreciated the overall rating, that I didn't understand some of her comments. I said that I didn't understand what was wrong with what I wore to school. The principal said that I should be dressing up on days she gives tours to families. I politely shared that I didn't know when tours were given and I wasn't aware that I was supposed to do that. The principal said I should ask for the tour schedule. Getting paid $21,000 a year and trying to afford an apartment in the city, I didn't have suits and fancy dresses at that time in my life. I wore khakis and collared shirts. I looked casual and professional. It was hard to swallow coming from a woman who wore large dresses, nylons and Birkenstocks each day, but nonetheless, I moved on.

The next thing I asked about was the comment that I needed to "bare more regard to safety issues." The principal said that it was against the rules to have electrical appliances in the classrooms. I told the principal that I had no idea what she was talking about. She said that the coffee pot on the counter by my desk was not acceptable. I was completely dumbfounded. I had yet to drink a cup of coffee in my life. Perhaps she was talking about the teacher next door to me who had not only a coffee pot, but an iron and a small microwave in her classroom. I was furious, yet knew I had to remain professional. I told her that I had no appliances in my classroom and would like it removed from my final evaluation. She said she would have to think about it.

Lastly, I proceeded to ask about "changing format on school-wide documents." The principal stated that without asking, I changed the format of the school progress report and sent it out to parents. I did so after asking her and receiving a note on my progress reports that said, "Great job on P/R," and she signed her name. She saw the changes I made. Or perhaps she didn't look at them. She said I did a great job. To me, that was the end of the story, but I guess not. I was embarrassed to hand out progress reports to parents that reflected nothing but negativity, so I made them more positive. Check out the comments on the progress report:

- Does not do well in daily work
- Low test scores
- Does not do requird work
- Does not do work on time
- Comes to class unprepared
- Fails to follow directions
- Fails to take initiative/Wastes time in class
- Does not participate in class discussions
- Fails to do neat/accurate work
- Fails to heed suggestions for improvement
- Misbehaves in the hallway during recess or after lunch
- Is restless and inattentive
- Poor Attitude
- Consistently disrupts class: too talkative
- Shows disrespect to authority
- Is rude and inconsiderate of others
- Frequent absence interferes with progress
- Often out of uniform
- Neglects personal appearance
- Frequently tardy

How horrible is that list? I crossed out the negative words to make the report positive. I had a room full of awesome kids

and I wasn't about to send home a report like that. If I had to do it all over again, I would have done the same thing.
This was my very first experience with teacher evaluation. In conclusion of that experience, she did nothing to help grow my teaching skills, however she did teach me what not to do as a future leader. Regardless of how difficult any situation may be, we certainly learn from all people in our lives. The most important thing about evaluation is that it is a tool to grow and common sense would tell us that we should use it as a tool to grow.

Common sense leaders celebrate the strengths in their teachers and help develop areas in need of improvement. The most amazing part of evaluation is conversation. The key to positive teacher evaluations is the relationship between the teacher and leader. Teachers are smart people. Most of them know where they need to improve or step it up. It is the job of a common sense leader to help teachers feel comfortable saying they need to improve or need help in certain areas. Proceed with caution, although because you will have teachers who think they are wonderful and they simply are not. That is where proper documentation, consistent, compassionate and serious conversations need to happen. It's never easy, but when kids get one shot, it makes common sense to accept only the very best for our children.

Along with inaccurate evaluations come the ghost evaluations. I also worked at a school where evaluations appeared out of thin air and were handed to the teacher on the way out the door on the last day of school. No discussion. No goals. Nothing. This helped me learn the difference between compliance and dedicated work. You see, some teachers may be fine with no discussion, no goals and no growth observation. Others, however, work hard, are effective and want the chance to talk about their practice. Evaluation is about everything in this book. It is about relationships, listening, understanding, high expectations, work ethic, culture and being organized.

Being an effective evaluator is not an easy task. Working hard to get into classrooms as much as possible with the tremendous amount of other tasks, is overwhelming. Gathering evidence is the best way to write a fair and appropriate evaluation. Guiding your teachers to understand what evidence means is half the battle. Helping people understand that this evaluation is not about you, but it is about your practice. The best message I give to teachers is that you can grow in your practice and I will help you. Enter those with their guards up. This is where evaluations take a turn. This is where you learn the most about your teachers. Will they listen and reflect on their practice or will they be defensive and upset. We have both in our schools. The difficult ones in defense mode are draining. The positive, self-reflecting ones are inspirational. I find honor in helping both, but I know in the end which ones will find success with kids.

Every teacher sets his or her path with their attitude. I just act as the guidance for individual and team growth. Remember, leadership is not a popularity contest. It is a serious path to help grow people.

I am the Master of my Fate and the Captain of my Soul...You are too.

"The culture of any organization is shaped by the worst behavior the leader is willing to tolerate."

- Todd Whitaker

8
Relationships

"Trust is the oxygen of our school systems. You can't see it, hear it, touch it, or feel it, but without it, you will find yourself struggling to survive."

-Shelley Burgess & Beth Houf

Building relationships with people is the **MOST** important part of leadership. People can see through phoney. When I meet someone, I can tell within five minutes if that person is full of it. That feeling is hard to get rid of as the conversation continues. We've all been there. You have a boss or colleague who you just don't trust. Think about it. Think about who they are, how they talk, how they treat you and others and what you feel about their character. It is impossible to work with people you do not trust. Well, it's possible, but it's not fun. Also know that no one is making you stay in a job that makes you feel rotten. Take charge of your life and go where you are appreciated, not tolerated. Common sense leaders work in many ways to build trusting relationships. Trusting relationships are the foundation to any successful opportunity.

Building trust with people starts with integrity and character. A common sense leader never forgets the steps she took to be where she is...A common sense leader is in the classroom learning and growing with the teacher. A common sense leader talks *with* people, not *at* people. A common sense leader works to get to know the person behind the teaching and realizes that teachers are mothers, fathers, students, widows, novice, seasoned, etc. There is a story behind every person who works in your building. The activity I shared in chapter 6 is so powerful in getting to know who your teachers really are. Building trusting relationships will allow you to get to know th real person behind the teaching mask. People act certain ways for a reason. Life throws some pretty tough things at people. Understanding your teachers and their journeys may help you gain perspective into why they do what they do and say what they say. Leadership is unique in that you have to differentiate how you lead. The more you learn about your teachers, the better you can facilitate their growth. New teachers need guidance in a different way than veteran teachers. There are also times when the new teachers outshine the veterans and usually it has to do with attitude or fearlessness. New teachers come to us fresh, excited and ready to change the world. Some new teachers come to us too eager and offend the veteran…enter the common sense leader. What an opportunity to build relationships with people. When you talk to them and listen to them and keep your word, the trusting relationship grows and grows. It takes time and effort, but it is so worth every minute. Think about how hard it is to have those difficult conversations about performance and attitude…if you build relationships with people, they aren't quite as difficult.

On a daily basis, leaders deal with situations that need trusting relationships in order to be successful. On top of greeting kids at the door, creating schedules, talking with parents, evaluating teachers, participating in and presenting at meetings, printing and studying student data, preparing reports, checking email, responding to email, stopping nosebleeds, talking a parent or teacher off the ledge, covering for a teacher who had a sick child, having fire drills, working through surprise lockdown drills, calling 911 for a student who had an asthma attack, and trying to get a bite to eat during lunch, a leader deals with endless issues. Don't allow the day-to-day craziness to get in the way of why you are the leader. When you feel overwhelmed, and you will, go back to your why. Take a walk. Get into classrooms. Eat lunch with kids. Call someone to tell them you appreciate their help. Call one of your cheerleaders to talk you off the ledge to remind you why you do what you do. Life is full of possibilities to lift us up when we feel down. You just have to remember your why in order to relight your passion. Live in every moment.

The job list is endless and if relationships are not built, it makes all of these situations much more difficult to deal with. I have worked with leaders who do not make life easier for their people because of the decisions they make. Some see teachers as teachers and nothing else. The truth is our job or career is a part of who we are, a big part. But common sense leadership sees beyond the job and into the person. People have lives, feelings, emotions and at the end of the day most people just want to do well. Leaders have the responsibility and opportunity to help make people successful.

I also believe very strongly that building relationships involves opening up your life to those you work with. I am open about the difficulties of juggling motherhood with a career. I am open with the stress, love and joy of raising children. I have seen the magic of people feeling comfortable just because they share that I put my pants on each morning just as they do. (Although why it is that the size keeps growing if I never get the chance to sit down to eat lunch? Hmm.) The key to building relationships with people is to be open, honest and humble. Talking with people about the stress of life, sharing their fears and accomplishments is powerful. I often look at my job as an opportunity to make life for people a little easier at times. Life is hard enough and you don't need a leader making it harder.

Those types of leaders are certainly out there though. Leaders who are not on the Clue Bus. I've had them and it's horribly disheartening, but I certainly learned from every one of them. Those who focus on the wrong things. Those who don't really care about people. Those who demand - those who expect respect - those who don't listen. Those who could truly care less about you and treat people like chess pieces. Unfortunately, there are a lot of leaders out there who are not using common sense. Leaders who don't build trust lead schools where frustration is high, teachers are salty and climate & culture are sour. Not good. Not productive. Not Common Sense Leadership.

"Stand close to people who feel like sunshine."

-Anonymous

9
CELEBRATIONS

"The more you praise and celebrate your life, the more there is in life to celebrate."

-Oprah Winfrey

Life is short. We talk about it all of the time. How did they get so big? Oh my goodness, how is he already graduating from high school? Retirement comes quick. Why not make the best of every single day?

Celebrating people and their accomplishments is a very common sense way to approach leadership. There are things in schools that can be celebrated all day long. In every classroom you have kids making progress, teachers growing in their craft, parents learning how amazing their children really are...it goes on and on. Why not recognize greatness? Celebrate the fact that we are alive, growing, thriving and we are doing it together.

The joy we can bring into the lives of our students, teachers and parents is endless. We just have to do it. Here are some ideas that have been successful in celebrating PEOPLE, the most important part of our jobs!

Social Media

Just like you, your school has a story and if you don't tell it, someone else, who may not have all of the information might. You live it daily, you see it daily and you help create it, so tell it! Social media is an awesome way to tell your story. It is also vital to stay connected to others in your shoes. Leadership can be a lonely position, but like Aaron Hogan says, "Twitter may not change your life, but the educators there will." Building your Professional Learning Network (PLN) and sharing your story will keep you fresh, make you feel proud and give you a place where you can share ideas and find people like you! An awesome resource for those just starting or veteran Twitter users is *140 Twitter Tips for Educators* by Brad Currie, Billy Krakower & Scott Rocco. Regardless of your expertise, this book will help with ideas!

Telling your school's story through social media will do several things for you. You are crazy busy, I know. Remember the list of things you do listed in chapter 8, well add 100 more to that, so anything we can do to work smarter, not harder is cool with me. Think about this for a minute: You are outside greeting students every morning, you are in the lunchroom, in classrooms, at school activities, participating in professional development, presenting awards to kids, listening to their music concerts, watching their amazingness on stage, etc. Why not capture those moments and share them out? Carry your phone, snap a picture and tweet it out. It sounds simple, because it is. If you are not familiar with Twitter or the many other social media outlets, no worries. We are all learners and we never stop. There are many books, like the one mentioned above, and videos for learning about social media. You will have students at school who know the ins and outs of social media better than all of us. Ask them. My guess would be that they would be honored to tell their principal how to use it. They may even have some ideas we haven't even thought of. That's why they are amazing.

Classroom observations, something that can take up a huge chunk of time, can also become more happy and positive with the use of social media. When in classrooms, snap pictures of the kids working, the teacher facilitating, the work assigned, the projects and the classroom environment. Take videos of the kids engaged in their thinking. You can not only tweet out the excellence in your classrooms, but you can also follow up with the teacher by sending her the pictures with a note regarding the observation. Whether a short walk through, an informal or a formal observation, the power of a picture will go a long way! Pictures really do say 1000 words and they are great conversation starters with teachers when discussing their craft and all of the thought behind it.

Some teachers will welcome pictures and some may feel "threatened" so asking them beforehand and sharing your plans with how you are going to use them will put people at ease. Once they see the positive attention it brings to sharing their awesomeness, it will be accepted by most. Remember, not all will accept or like everything you do, but again this is not a popularity contest. Whatever is best for the kids, the teachers and the community rules. Kids first always. Tell your story and be **#CelebratED**!

Community News

How often do you call the local newspaper or news media to cover an event at your school? People need to see what you are doing, because you are growing young lives and making a difference in this world every day. Perhaps your kids are participating in a wax museum or building out-of-this-world STEM projects. You need to tell people. Call the local media and ask if they would like to cover a story at your school. How about the mayor, state representatives, local business people? They should know too and this is a great way to build up relationships in your community. When you have a speaker or school assembly or have the kids get to throw a pie in your face because they reached a reading goal, call someone and tell them! How about a teacher who won an award? Celebrate him/her! The more our society hears about the importance of what we do, the better off we will be. Tell your story and be **#CelebratED**!

Student Achievements

There is nothing more joyful that experiencing the success of a child. Whether academic or social/emotional, we are in the business of growing kids and it is the most important thing in the world. Think about how you celebrate their achievements. Do you have assemblies honoring kids? Monthly, quarterly, annually...do they know the why behind their honors and their growth? Are students involved in honoring their peers and teachers involved in honoring each other? Do you invite parents to see their kids being recognized? There are endless possibilities to honor kids...

→ acts of kindness

→ academic growth and/or achievement
→ leadership roles in the school
→ service
→ sports
→ the arts
→ local, state or national contests

Tell your story and provide opportunities for kids to be
#CelebratED!

Birthdays

Everyone has one so why not make them special? For students,
they could come to your office for a pencil, book, certificate or
credits to the school store. You and your office staff could sing
to him/her. You could have a special monthly lunch for
birthday kids. All of these options are simple ways to get to
know the kids personally. School is their home away from
home and for some, their safe place. For your teachers and staff,
how about an extra plan period, a monthly recognition
celebration, a shoutout or a $5 gift card? Recognition of all
kinds build relationships that are significant to your school's
story! Make sure kids and adults get **#CelebratED**!

Clothing

If you look around, you will see so many fun and positive
messages on children's clothing these days. Comment on it.
Tell him how cool his shirt is. If it says "World Changer," tell
him you know he is a world changer and you can't wait to see
what his future holds. Take a picture and tweet it out telling the
world about your school's message. Wendy Hankins
(@MrsHankinsClass), an innovative 2nd grade teacher at

@KirkElementary in Houston, Texas will be starting #WiseWordWednesday at her school this year. The goal is to have students and staff wear positive words on their shirts every Wednesday and it will be celebrated throughout the day. All of these personal connections with the kids help build those relationships that are the foundation to successful experiences with them. All kids should be **#CelebratED**!

Calling Home

A huge highlight for me is calling parents with the student present. When I'm in classrooms and I see something really cool, I react to it. It could be an act of kindness by a child, an academic realization or a child sharing out when she is usually quiet. I ask the child to take a little walk and we go call home. Talk about bringing joy and sharing our story. The kid is smiling ear to ear and the parent's pride is beaming through the phone. You want to make an impact on your students and parents? Call and tell their parents how awesome their kids are. Be specific and make sure they know how proud you are. Another way to build those ever so important relationship that are the foundation to all things success! Calling home is a way to make sure kids and parents are **#CelebratED**!

Just Because

Celebrating kids, teachers and parents can happen all of the time. The way you treat others, interact with them and leave them feeling IS celebrating. Your core values come out in everything you say and everything you do. Your words and actions leave an impression on everyone you meet. You can make or break the day other others, so spread goodness everywhere! Check out these ideas:

★ Dress up in your mascot at arrival with a sign that says, I'm so glad you're here!

★ Take a test with your kids and share that whomever meets or beats your score gets to have a special lunch with you. Have the kids "tutor" you on the problems you got incorrect.

★ Read the book a group is reading and participate in the book study!

★ Have a dance-off in the halls or at lunch.

★ Frame pictures of your students, teachers and parents throughout the hallways of your school. What better to decorate with but the faces you are inspiring every day.

★ Put positive messages on your letter or electronic signs outside of your school. A great way to spread what you want people to know about your school.

★ Host a BOOk Fair where families bring in a pumpkin they carved of a character in their favorite book!

★ Paint the ceiling tiles at your school! It could be your school theme, motivational quotes or paintings done by students.

★ Host Lunch with a Loved One where every child gets to bring a special adult and sit out in the school yard for lunch. A blanket, picnic basket and a whole lot of love!

★ What about Taste of "Your School" where families get to bring dishes honoring their cultures.

The possibilities are truly endless and let the sky be your limit!

#CelebratED

As I mentioned before, the power of a Professional Learning Network (PLN) is unbelievable. Every Wednesday evening at 8:30 PM CST, our PLN celebrates the journey of education, and all of the people who make it happen on Twitter. Our group is made up of 15 people from 11 states! We are teachers, curriculum coaches, consultants, reading specialists, school counselors, assistant principals, principals and superintendents. The power of a group to communicate together, support each other and gain different perspectives is truly an amazing experience. Each week we co-lead a topic to #CelebratED and help others grow in their craft. Doing what's best for kids and taking care of each other are vital to success. I hope you join us on Wednesday nights!

"Your words and actions leave a lasting impression everywhere you go. Make sure they sparkle!"

-Heidy LaFleur

10
It's Up to You

"Teachers affect eternity; no one can tell where their influence stops."

-Henry Brooks Adams

Well, it's up to you. You can join me on the Clue Bus, or you can stand at the bus stop. Those on the Clue Bus make things happen. They set goals & high expectations and guide their teachers to success. They sacrifice time and energy for the good of their teams and most of all lead by example. Those on the Clue Bus make a difference each and every day. As you reflect on your leadership style, think about who you are. Think about your core beliefs. If you have never taken a moment to write out your core beliefs, do so. It is a very powerful mental organization of your thoughts. As I tell my own children, your mind will believe whatever you tell it. If your true core beliefs are at the forefront of all that you do, your leadership will thrive. You, as a leader, will grow more than ever if you are on that organized path. Reflecting on your practice is vital to your growth. Remember that not everyone will like you. Remember that you are not alone, even though you may feel like it at times. Remember to listen to others stories and share yours too!

I asked all of the faculty and staff that I have ever worked with to write a paragraph describing what, in their eyes, makes an effective leader. I asked that they add their position and age to see if there is a difference in what novice and veteran teachers want in a leader. Here are the results:

Kindergarten Teacher, 50 years old

In my many years of teaching, I have come to realize that administrators can choose to look for the negative or look for the positive in each teacher. If you look hard enough, you can find something negative about any one of us. After all, we are human. However, it only takes a moment to see many good characteristics in teachers. Teachers all have strengths that can be shared with others. We don't all have to be excellent at everything. We simply need to be excellent at sharing what we are excellent at! We all strive to do our best in a positive, supportive environment with an administrator that believes in all we can be and continue to strive to be. A motivating, supportive administrator encourages teachers to grow professionally among peers. Teachers who feel supported will naturally be motivated and therefore motivate their students and teach with excellence. We all choose to educate students in order to truly make a difference. Why then wouldn't an administrator choose to provide a positive atmosphere with productive teamwork? After all, it only takes a brief moment to see the positive in every one of us!

Grade 1 Teacher, 25 years old

Honestly, I just need someone who believes in me. A good leader listens to my ideas and allows me to take risks. I know I am going to makes mistakes and a good leader helps me up and tells me to keep going. A good leader understands and never forgets what it's like to be in the classroom.

Digital Literacy Teacher, 30 years old

A good leader supports me and trusts me to do the job I was hired to do. A good leader is present and leads by example. A good leader delegates and isn't afraid to ask for help when he or she doesn't know the answer. A good leader inspires me to be a better educator. A good leader cultivates a positive work environment and encourages collaboration. The knowledge that my leader has the aforementioned traits allows me to take risks, thus, growing my students in and out of the classroom. A great leader motivates me to arrive each day with a smile and makes me want to be the best educator I can be. Even if *I* can't accomplish something; I know *we* can!

Language Arts Teacher, 43 years old
This type of leader encourages and even at times when necessary, *insists* that teachers plan, plan, and plan some more. Good teachers can "wing it," but even those most seasoned teachers do a better job when they are required to write detailed lesson plans and be accountable for what is going on in their classroom each day. When given too much freedom, even the best of workers (in any job) will slack. An effective leader has somewhat high expectations for those he/she leads. In addition, an effective leader shows appreciation for hard work which encourages more hard work and reciprocal appreciation. Lastly, an effective leader delegates rather than micromanaging.

Junior High Science Teacher, 39 years old
Having worked under five principals, I have had different experiences. I grew as a teacher the most under the leadership of one principal. During this time, I felt like my grade level and principal were part of a team with a clear vision. When we met, we discussed curriculum and how to best get things done—and we took action. Moreover, we all held each other in the highest respect and felt like family. As a family, we supported and encouraged each other to try new things or find new strategies.

With her hard work and enthusiasm, you wanted to be part of her team.

Kindergarten Teacher, 27 years old
A leader works to support and encourage all those around her. She helps by offering guidance, a fresh perspective and new ideas. With a unique way of approaching teaching, a leader can inspire change in other educators around her. By "shaking things up", a leader once guided me to revamp my English Language Arts and guided reading curriculum. After doing so, my students were more engaged learners and had a better understanding of our standards. It was AWESOME to see! Leaders encourage you to work that much harder to see results and it makes the growth even more rewarding!

Grade 6 Teacher, 46 years old
The most important characteristic I find in a leader that helps me be the very best teacher I can be is the ability to listen. If I am going to this leader - there is a really strong reason. I need to be heard. From that listening there can be all sorts of angles: empathy, advice, guidance but this needs to be done in a professional/respectful manner. And if I am out of line/wrong, tell me. I will work hard on fixing it. The best leaders lead by example. If you want me to do something, the leader also needs to be doing it. Most leaders come from the classroom and work their way up. There are a lot of new responsibilities that make a leader forget what it was like dealing with the day-to-day "petty classroom things" that wear a teacher down. What seems like no big deal might take a lot of my time to complete. If I am spending time on the paperwork, the students suffer. When I am at the end of my rope, step in and help me. I obviously need it. These are the things that will then trickle down to the

students and make me a better teacher, and therefore them, better students - socially, emotionally or academically.

Grade 5 Teacher, 39 years old
A good leader has many qualities, but patience, confidence, effective communication, and drive stand out to me. Also, someone who is constantly growing and evolving themselves makes a good leader. If you see their drive and motivation, it pushes you to keep moving and growing and doing your best. Other characteristics include being passionate and supportive. Good leaders state clear expectations and communicate their vision with their staff. I also think having high expectations (within reason) is important because it promotes growth and crushes stagnancy. These qualities can all be transferred into the classroom with students. Having high expectations placed upon me, causes me to have high expectations with my students. Being patient, passionate about teaching, and communicating clearly and effectively hopefully influences my students positively. If students see me working hard and valuing growth and learning, then hopefully that will translate into something meaningful in their educational career.

Classroom Teacher, 37 years old
I believe effective principals set standards and expectations, but also allow freedom and art in how those expectations and standards are met. When the standards are set there is no room for uncertainty. As a leader the principal encourages the teachers to achieve and exceed the expectations using the individual teacher strengths, the collaborative strengths of the staff, and also provides opportunities for professional growth and development in areas which need further refinement. It is important that the principal build a strong, POSITIVE

community. Often the teachers have established communities with peers, or grade level partners. It is a principal who provides the foundations of an entire school community. The school environment needs to be welcoming and warm for the staff and the students. Effective principals develop positive relationships with the staff as a whole and each teacher individually. I believe positive attitudes towards growth and development allow students to grow. Recognizing the small successes, as well as, the large ones is an important factor in developing students. The principal should create positive relationships with the students. The students need to know and see the principal as a part of their educational journey. The children need to be encouraged by the principal and the principal should recognize successes (whether it be by note, comment on report card, or speaking with the child). I believe the principal should encourage and celebrate growth as a student in academics and growth as a person in their character. It is important that the teachers and principal promote lifelong learners through curriculum, experiences and a sense of community.

Early Childhood Special Education Teacher, 48 years old
I can be the very best teacher that I can be when I work with a leader that shares a mutual respect with me. I automatically have a certain level of respect for my leader because of her position, her education, and her experience. That respect will grow over time as we work together. I understand that my leader and I will not always agree, but we must be respectful of our individual positions. At the same time, I expect to be treated with a certain level of respect because of my position, education, and experience. The respect that I receive from my leader fosters an environment of collaboration with her. We can discuss matters, both big and small, and know that we both

want a solution that is appropriate. Ultimately, we share a common goal and our ability to work together professionally allows me to accomplish all that I need to do.

Grade 4 Teacher, 36 years old

A leader that listens is a very important quality to have. I want a leader that truly listens to my concerns, fears, struggles, ideas and celebrations. When a leader does that, I feel valued and that my job matters. Teaching is really hard when done effectively and I appreciate when a leader recognizes that.

Grade 5 Teacher, 29 years old

To me an effective leaders is someone I can go to and share ideas with. Someone who can help me be the best I can be and definitely someone who trusts me. I also believe the most effective leaders are in classrooms never forgetting what it's like to be a teacher. I appreciate a leader who is compassionate and knows that I have a family at home, as well as my family at school.

Reading Specialist, 35 years old

A leader that helps me be my best is a person who provides the structure and environment that allows for collaboration and teamwork with colleagues and provides the time, resources and information I need to help my students. Someone who has an open door policy for conversations with staff and is realistic and understanding about life both in and outside of school helps as well.

6-8 General/Vocal Music Teacher, 53 years old

I find that a person who backs me up when dealing with students, especially with discipline issues, helps me to be an effective teacher. This is particularly important when in front of the students. An effective leader would talk with me privately if they had an issue with the way I handled things and give me constructive (not condescending) suggestions on ways to handle the situation differently in the future. I also would like a leader to acknowledge and appreciate the work that is put into a lesson or activity.

Art Teacher Grades K-8, 44 years old
I think that leaders must lead by example. If we want students to trust us enough to confide in us and help the "whole child" grow, (which gives them confidence in their learning), leaders must find ways to build trust with these students as well. They need to not be afraid to let children know that they are humans that make mistakes too. They hurt and feel joy just like they do. They need to show balance. "All work and no play makes Johnny a dull boy!" If a leader brings fun (for everyone, not just a select few) to the workplace, I feel you are more inclined to respond when it's time to get serious and get work done!

Middle School Teacher, 36 Years Young
Leaders are in a sense coaches. A good coach prepares you for the task at hand. When you face adversity, a good coach recognizes your struggle and provides you the knowledge, skill, and opportunity to overcome that struggle. In addition, win or lose, a good coach acknowledges your effort and commitment to the program and understands that we are in this as a team. This allows me to translate my coaching onto the students.

Grade 4 Teacher, 54 years old
What I find the best in a leader would be compassion and fairness. I rank compassion first because an understanding leader with compassion would motivate me to change or stride for higher understanding in my field. As humans, we need

understanding and a connection to a leader. I like a leader who is committed to guidance and leadership to get me on the right path to be the best teacher I can be.

Assistant Principal, 36 years old
Characteristics that I find in a leader who helps me to be the very best I can be include being a good listener when I have doubts, being supportive when I need encouragement and being the safety net between me and parents when needed. The leader who has these characteristics allows for student growth in and out of the classroom because the teacher feels supported and confident in what they are doing and instill those feelings into their students.

Here it is in black and white. They are sharing what they need from us. Listen to them. Go make a difference. No questions, no complaints, no excuses. Just do it and do it well. Be awesome. I hope you decide to join me on the Clue Bus. You **CAN** and **WILL** make a difference if you take a seat. All the best on your common sense journey!

"Every child deserves a champion: an adult who will never give up on them, who understands the power of connection and insists they become the best they can possibly be."

-Rita Pierson

About the Author

Heidy LaFleur is a vibrant, positive and common sense leader with explosive passion for helping people achieve greatness. She has been a teacher and school administrator working in education since 2000. Heidy is now the CEO of Common Sense Leadership, LLC in which she provides inspirational speaking, education consulting and leadership coaching. She is a grateful wife of a firefighter/paramedic and proud mother of three beautiful children. In 2016, she was awarded the Double D Award from Drake University which is the highest honor bestowed on alumni student-athletes for work in their field of study.

About the Author

I'd like to tell you about the author of this book, my mom. She is a loving, caring, encouraging and awesome mom. She comes home every day and asks us about our days. She is very supportive to me and my brothers. My mom attends all of our school events and sporting activities. She tells us that the most important thing is family and to never give up. Every time we get out of the car, she tells us to have good manners, to have fun and to do your best. My mom is the best mom I could ever have! – Lilly LaFleur, Age 11 (First Edition)

Contact Heidy for your next event!

I am **Heidy with a WHY**.

Let me help you be the best you can be.

"The two most important days in your life are the day you are born and the day you find out why."

-Mark Twain

Made in the USA
Monee, IL
11 October 2022

15653177R10057